LONDON & NORTH WESTERN RAILWAY

Opening of the

# STALBRIDGE DOCK,

# GARSTON

February 24th, 1909.

# London & North Western Railway.

# GARSTON DOCKS.

## Opening of "Stalbridge" Dock

### BY

## The Rt. Hon. Lord STALBRIDGE, P.C.

**Mr. FRANK REE,**
**General Manager.**

THE NEW STALBRIDGE DOCK IN THE MAKING.

GENERAL VIEW OF THE OPERATIONS.

3

THE NEW STALBRIDGE DOCK (GENERAL VIEW).

SECTIONAL VIEW OF NEW STALBRIDGE DOCK, SHEWING LOCK LEADING TO RIVER AND ALSO COMMUNICATION PASSAGE LEADING TO OLD DOCK.

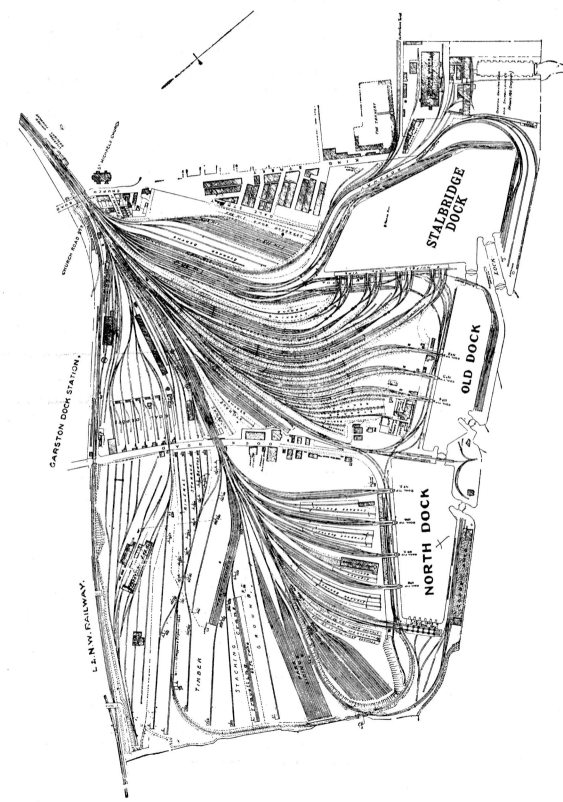

SKETCH OF GARSTON DOCKS AND ESTATE

(INCLUDING NEW STALBRIDGE DOCK AND EXTENDED STORAGE ACCOMMODATION FOR TIMBER, MINERAL ORES, &C.)

6

SECTIONAL VIEW OF STALBRIDGE DOCK, SHEWING 30 TON HYDRAULIC COAL HOISTS.

GRADIENT SIDINGS LEADING TO STALBRIDGE DOCK.

8

VIEW OF NORTH DOCK (FROM NORTH END) SHEWING COMMUNICATION PASSAGE LEADING TO THE OLD DOCK.

VIEW OF NORTH DOCK (FROM SOUTH END).

VIEW OF OLD DOCK (FROM EAST SIDE).

11

TWO NEW MOVEABLE HYDRAULIC COAL HOISTS AT NORTH DOCK,
EACH OF 30 TONS CAPACITY, FITTED WITH ANTI-BREAKAGE APPLIANCES, AND END DOORS ON CHUTES MECHANICALLY CONTROLLED BY
OPERATOR.    BOTH HOISTS CAN BE USED FOR ONE STEAMER AT THE SAME TIME.

FOUR SIMILAR TIPS HAVE BEEN ERECTED AT THE NEW STALBRIDGE DOCK.

# Garston Docks.

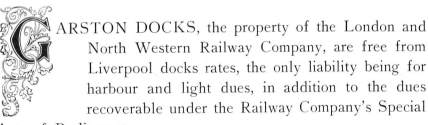

GARSTON DOCKS, the property of the London and North Western Railway Company, are free from Liverpool docks rates, the only liability being for harbour and light dues, in addition to the dues recoverable under the Railway Company's Special Acts of Parliament.

Garston is recognised as a cheap port, both for shipowners and merchants, consequently its resources are continually taxed. Under these conditions the London and North Western Railway Company some time ago obtained powers for the construction of a third dock, and this extension, to be opened to-day, will practically double the existing berthing accommodation. Additional sidings and storage grounds to an even greater ratio have also been provided.

Being a railway port, goods are naturally transferred direct from ship to railway wagon, or vice versa, thus reducing handling and obviating costly cartage, advantages representing a great saving to merchants.

At the present time vessels up to 5,000 tons carrying capacity can be dealt with at the port, but when the new channel is complete (probably about the end of the year) it will be accessible to vessels of 10-12,000 tons. This channel, about 800 yards long and 300 feet wide, leads direct from the Garston Deeps to the new Stalbridge Dock entrance.

This important development will put a stop to the drawback caused by large vessels arriving in the Mersey on neap tides, and then having to lie in the river until the higher tides serve.

During 1907 the vessels clearing totalled :—

Steamers ... ... ... ... 3,980
Sailing vessels ... ... ... 480
Lighters ... ... ... ... 4,110

The Company has laid down a complete electrical installation sufficient to light the dock entrances, coal tips, quays, wharves, sidings, and storage area, as well as the extensive new shunting and marshalling yard at Speke. This scheme for improved lighting should be of considerable benefit to ship-owners and others, as the work of loading and discharging at night will be expedited thereby, the intention being to provide portable arc lamps for use in the holds of vessels wherever the nature of cargo will admit.

In addition to the many facilities provided by the Company in their efforts to make the port complete in all equipment, it should be mentioned that tenancy facilities have been granted on their estate whereby engineers, ship store dealers, repairing shops, etc., are brought conveniently near, to the benefit of steamship owners who wish to take advantage of the loading or discharging days in order to effect slight repairs, alterations, etc., without causing additional delays to vessels.

## NAVIGATION SOUTH OF LIVERPOOL.

The channel from Liverpool is indicated by red buoys on the starboard hand and black buoys on the port hand. There is a beacon off Dingle Point with a flashing red light, showing two flashes about every 10 seconds. The western extremity of Pluckington Bank is marked by a black can gas bell-buoy with a flashing red light. Light-ship situated at Otterspool.

This provides a channel of 35 feet deep, varying in width from 430 feet to 950 feet, based on a mean tide level 15 feet above old dock sill, Liverpool, *vide* 1906 survey.

The approaches are well defined, leading lights (green) being fixed on the north side of the entrance to the north dock, and on the high level in the rear, to assist masters and pilots when navigating in the dark.

## PILOTAGE.

The same compulsory pilotage services which apply to vessels entering or leaving all ports on the Mersey are available in connection with the docks, viz. : that controlled and regulated by the Mersey Docks and Harbour Board.

## TUGS.

With regard to towing facilities the various tug companies which work in conjunction with the Liverpool, Birkenhead, and Runcorn docks, and the Ship Canal, will also serve the docks; and tug boats of different sizes and power are available practically day or night.

## DOCK DUES.

All vessels entering the North Dock pay 2d. per ton dock dues on net register, while vessels entering the Old Dock pay 3d. per ton on quantity of cargo discharged and/or loaded, except in the case of coal exported, upon which at present no dues are levied.

The dock dues in the new Stalbridge Dock will be 4d. per ton on the vessel's registered tonnage, except in regard to vessels arriving in ballast, and loading outwards with coal or coke, which will be liable to pay to the Company dock dues of 3d. per ton upon their registered tonnage.

## DOCK ACCOMMODATION.

|  | Width of entrance. feet. | Depth of water on sill. Spring. feet. | Depth of water on sill. Neap. feet. | Water area. acres. | Berthing space. feet. |
|---|---|---|---|---|---|
| **North Dock** ... | 55 | 28 | 18 | 8 | 2,400 |
| **Old Dock** ... ... | 50 | 25 | 15 | 6 | 2,160 |
| **Stalbridge Dock** ... | 65 with a lock 276 feet long. | 33 | 26 | 14½ | 3,170 |

Communication passages exist between the North and Old Docks, and a further communication between the Old and (new) Stalbridge Dock, 65 feet wide has been constructed. Any craft suitable for the new lock will thus be able to enter or leave either of the docks approximately from two to three hours before and after high water.

CRANES.

**North Dock**— Sheerlegs, 40 tons capacity ; 13 portable hydraulic cranes with lifting capacity 30 to 50 cwts.

**Old Dock**—15 portable hydraulic cranes with lifting capacity 30 to 50 cwts.; 1 hand crane, 10 tons.

**The Stalbridge Dock**—16 portable hydraulic cranes with lifting capacity 50 cwts. ; 2 portable hydraulic cranes with lifting capacity 4 tons.

COALING FACILITIES.

**North Dock**—Two moveable hydraulic tips each of 30 tons capacity, fitted with anti-breakage appliances, and end doors on chutes mechanically controlled by operator. Both tips can be used for one boat at the same time. Four fixed high level tips.

**Old Dock**—Three fixed high level tips.

**Stalbridge Dock**—Four moveable hydraulic tips, each of 30 tons capacity, fitted with anti-breakage appliances, the same as those in the North Dock. These tips will be capable of tipping coal into vessels at any height up to 45 feet from quay level, and arrangements have been designed so as to permit of two or even three tips being utilised for one vessel at one time.

The large hydraulic tips provided at the Stalbridge Dock as well as the two already in use in the North Dock, accommodate the larger type of coal wagons of 15 to 20 tons carrying capacity, which colliery proprietors and others are beginning to appreciate as more economical to work. A number of these wagons have been regularly working to and from Garston since the advent of the two large hydraulic tips in the North Dock.

## WAREHOUSE AND STORAGE.

Extensive Warehouse accommodation exists in connection with the Docks, and further provision will be made, as circumstances may require, to meet developments in the Stalbridge Dock.

## MINERAL STORAGE BERTHS.

A very large business in minerals is conducted through this port, viz., sulphur, copper, manganese, iron, and other ores.

The Company has provided " floored " berths of a special character, and accommodation now exists on these berths for upwards of 100,000 tons of mineral cargo.

The import of minerals during 1907 was 391,553 tons.

The Company has just provided special premises adequately fitted with appliances for the purposes of sampling mineral ores, a convenience very highly appreciated by the merchants and analytical chemists who are engaged in determining values.

## TIMBER STORAGE BERTHS.

There are about 48 acres of storage ground especially levelled and provided with sidings at convenient distances from each other, so as to admit of cargoes being laid down, sorted, piled or selected as may be necessary.

Special accommodation for heavy logs has been provided, and a travelling crane is available for stacking, etc., which is capable of piling logs to a height of 30 feet.

## TOTAL TONNAGE.

| | 1907. |
|---|---|
| Imports ... ... ... ... | 666,011 |
| Exports (including coal) ... | 2,738,131 |
| | 3,404,142 |

## REGULAR SAILINGS.

There are regular weekly sailings from Garston Docks to Rouen, Bordeaux, and other French ports by Messrs. the Co-operative Wholesale Society's and Messrs. J. P. Hutchinson's, Glasgow (Messrs. R. J. Francis & Co., Liverpool Agents), steamers.

## RAILWAYS.

The London and North Western Railway Company are owners, and therefore control the entire working of the docks, which are, of course, directly connected with their main line system—and through the latter with the systems of all the railway companies in the country.

There are some 70 miles of sidings at the port, of which 8 miles are actually on or alongside the quays, and therefore available for direct working of cargoes from ship side to trucks or vice versa.